Braving the Storm:

Life's Cleansing Moments

Joyful Highs + Destructive Lows= Life

Table of Contents

"Emotional tidal waves occur within us all. It doesn't matter if the moment is a sad or happy occasion, it's the struggle within the storm that defines and builds character."

-Danielle L. Bigsby

New Beginnings

Possibilities

Endless possibilities when it comes to love,

Endless opportunities at joy,

All you search for in life is happiness,

If only you were given the chance.

If only you were given the chance to put a smile on

someone else's face,

Ecstasy is all you want,

Just one pure taste.

Happily ever after is what you dream of,

But you must wait until God sends you your one true

love.

The possibilities are endless if you just wait,

As long as God's in it,

It's never too late!

Dream Big

Dream big,

Never settle for something small,

But always remember,

In order to walk,

You must first crawl.

Dream big,

Go out and accomplish what you set out to do,

A dream is nothing without effort,

So in order to get it done,

You got to move.

Dream big,

Write down your vision and make it plain,

You must stay on course,

And realize along the way,

People will change.

Dream big,

And don't let anything stop you,

The only way a dream can become reality is with you!

He Who Completes

What a day it will be,

When I can say,

He's mine,

All mine.

The one sent to protect me,

To hold me,

To inspire me,

To revive me.

To treat me like a Queen,

And respect my mind, body, and soul,

To repair my heart,

Piece by piece,

Until it's whole.

To encourage my strengths,

And build up my weaknesses,

To help uncover my full potential,

And push me to continue to reach for the stars.

The one who's smile brings nothing but joy,

No more tears,

Nothing but smiles.

Oh,

What a day it will be once he enters my life,

Everything will be complete,

And finally,

My mind will be at peace at night.

Never Stop

When your back's against the wall,

And you just want to give up,

You see no way out,

But you can't stop.

Heart's hurting from all the pain,

Everything crumbling all around you,

Your life seems to be falling apart,

Don't stop.

Children acting a fool,

No support from your significant other,

Family acting strange,

But don't quit.

Bills due,

But money's funny,

Car out of gas,

And you're down to your last.

Eyes full of tears,

Mind troubled with worries and fears,

Where can you go?

What can you do?

Who can you turn to?

Exhale,

Breathe,

Step back,

Is what I suggest,

For my God says this is only a test.

Will you run to me?

Or will you continue to stress?

Give it over to Him,

He will put your mind at rest.

Storms are always brewing,

And His hardest battles are given to His strongest warriors,

For when it rains,

It pours,

When it's thundering and lightening,

The sun is just waiting to shine.

So,

You must hold on,

You must withstand the wind,

And the rain,

The lightening,

And the storm.

Stand strong,

Stand tall,

Endure until the end,

For blessings are waiting,

He's ready to release,

But this trial,

You must beat.

So never stop,

Journey on,

And I guarantee,

You'll come out strong!

Inspiration

If you never dream,

Then you can never fail.

But you will have never accomplished anything,

And your story would be a lot less interesting to tell.

So you must start somewhere,

Pick something you love,

We are all blessed with gifts sent from above.

There is a unique something that speaks only to you,

It ignites your heart with passion,

And drives you to become the best you.

Search your soul,

Look deep within,

And only then can a new understanding begin.

So take this moment,

Inspire yourself,

Follow your dreams,

Give it your all until you have nothing left.

What You Think You Want

What you think you want,

May not be what you really need.

That man that once looked so good,

Gave you a world of drama.

And now you want to turn back the hands of time,

If only you could.

That baby that he told you he wants,

Turned into eighteen years of raising them on your own.

Being that millionaire you dreamed of,

Turned out to be more stress and confusion,

When you thought it would bring happiness and love.

See,

What you think you want,

Will never be what you need,

If God's not in the plan.

For God blesses us,

Yet we still desire the things of another man.

Take "you" out and put God in,

And that's when great things in your life shall begin.

He's Working

Miracles are still happening every day,

My God reveals himself in various ways.

You don't believe me,

Well listen to what I say…

He woke me up this morning,

He clothed me in my right mind,

There was food on my table,

My children woke up this morning,

He gave me common sense to know the battle is His,

Not mine.

He got me to church safely,

He gave me a mouth to praise Him,

And a hand to write these words.

So many miracles in one day,

I don't have enough time to write,

I know He's working,

How do I know,

Because I see Him working in my life.

<u>Letting Go</u>

Why is letting go so hard to do,

I have always been told that it's your past that shapes you,

And makes up the identity of you.

But when your past is full of hurt and pain,

It scars you and how to love again,

Your heart has to be retrained.

You want to open up and let people in,

But where to start,

And how to begin?

So you carry around this extra baggage all your life,

Wondering why you just can't get it right.

Love from the mother who birthed you,

You have never felt,

Only wanting love and acceptance from her and nothing else.

So because she didn't love you,

You don't know how to love yourself,

You keep reaching out,

But you don't truly know how to ask for help.

Repeating the same cycle time and time again,

Trying to find love in different men.

Each time feeling lower and lower,

Wanting to find love more and more.

Seeing people in their different relationships and wanting to

imitate what I see,

But not realizing,

That each person is different and what they have may not be

for me.

Before you can love someone else,

You have to first love yourself.

But in order to make progress,

You have to start to step away from the past,

You must learn from it,

But you can't continue to live in the hurt,

It's time to reveal your raw, true self,

Time to take off the mask,

And escape from the past.

It is truly hard to let go of the hurt,

But you must do this to uncover your true self worth.

Open your eyes and heart,

Let it all out,

You can voice how you feel straight from your mouth.

Write it down,

Just to get it out of your heart and mind,

Slowly but surely,

Your heart will get better in time.

Don't carry around your hurt for too long,

Because you can't handle this problem on your own.

The process of letting go is grueling and slow,

But once you begin,

It will truly show.

Your heart will smile from deep within,

And the process of loving yourself can finally begin.

So start letting go,

Piece by piece,

And over time,

Your heart will feel complete.

Discovering Me

Maturity

It begins when you realize that there are more important

people in life than just you,

It begins when you put away childish things and make

decisions like grownups do.

It begins as you begin to grow and realize that you don't

know as much as you think you know,

See,

Once you reach this point,

You are truly beginning to grow.

Maturity is the first sign of being an adult,

Respect from others will be the end result.

In adulthood will you thrive,

And remember,

Maturity is a process and it will continue for the rest of our

lives.

Unraveled

Unravel the layers of me,

And you will begin to see,

That I'm quite complicated,

And lots of issues lie beneath the surface.

I am a woman of many emotions,

And I wear them like a sleeve,

Words pierce my heart,

And like a wound to flesh,

It begins to bleed.

Fighting back tears,

While picking myself up time and time again,

I don't know how I continue to press on,

But somehow,

I exhibit an amazing amount of strength.

It surprises me,

How much I can actually endure,

My kids are my reason for holding on,

Of that I'm sure,

Life continuously knocks me down,

But I will always get back up fighting,

And continue to come back for more.

She's Beautiful

She's beautiful,

Both inside and out,

From the way she switches her legs,

To the way she speaks out loud.

She's beautiful,

Even though she's a little on the plus side,

Her curves fit her well,

Her outward appearance reflects her beauty hidden deep

inside.

She's beautiful,

She has to constantly remind herself,

Until she begins to feel what she speaks,

And her inner beauty peaks.

She's beautiful,

She says,

And smiles with so much confidence,

I'm that beautiful woman,

And regardless of what anyone else thinks,

My beauty has been known to place some in a trance,

A deep trance,

And imagine images of me,

While enjoying a nice, hard, stiff drink.

The Journey

Day 1,

Seems so easy,

It's not hard to give it up,

But by day 7,

You're yearning to be touched.

But to go backwards would cause you nothing but turmoil,

So you journey on,

Your body craves sex,

But your heart wants much more.

Discovering that you are more than the sums of your body

parts,

Desperately holding on,

Determined not to relive your past.

By day 30,

Things start to click,

And you realize you can do this.

Stopping the opposite sex's hidden agenda from the start,

While all along,

Repairing your heart.

Day 37,

And you're finding your self worth,

No more booty calls and late night flings,

Enduring and pressing your way until God sends your King.

And as you continue on,

You will know,

That no man deserves your body without a ring.

You are a jewel,

Precious and unique,

Let your future husband discover your body's mystique.

The Makings of Me

Who am I?

A complicated mess,

Or

A beautiful work of art?

Who am I?

A mother,

A leader,

A teacher,

A work in progress,

Or

A voice hidden behind other's actions?

Who am I?

A fierce, sexy woman unwilling to settle,

Or

A timid woman who hides behind her own shadow?

Who am I?

A God fearing, praying woman,

Or

One who's afraid to open her mouth?

Who am I?

I am a living, breathing, walking testimony.

I am a dedicated, loving mother.

I am a woman who loves herself.

I am a woman who knows her worth.

I am God's child.

Who am I?

At first I didn't know,

But I'm truly thankful ad grateful for growth.

I Once Existed

I once existed so that you may learn to become a better you,

You see,

I was wild with no regard for human life,

Partying,

Drinking,

Smoking,

Popping pills,

Only living life for my next thrill.

Although there was no method to my madness,

There was a reason for it all.

I once existed,

So that later on in life,

I could be your example of how to get right.

I once existed,

So that growth could occur,

I once existed,

So you would no longer have to wonder who you were.

Through me you lived and made many mistakes,

But I only existed,

So that later on,

Your life would be great.

Jagged Edges

Who am I?

Where did I come from?

Why am I not accepted?

Why don't they love me?

A lonely child,

Longing to be loved,

Confused by my outward appearance,

Afraid to express my inner feelings.

Why don't I look like you?

Why is my last name different?

Will you ever answer my questions?

Can I handle the truth?

Searching for answers,

And finally I get some,

But I wasn't ready,

I was truly stunned.

I was being raised by a legal guardian,

Had been since three weeks old,

According to her,

I was better off,

If truth be told.

But I wanted to know,

How could she walk away?

I am her child for goodness sake!

And where was my dad?

The man who created me,

You're better off,

See,

He's a junkie.

But I still wanted to know my roots,

What was my heritage?

So a reunion was set,

And we finally meet.

But soon,

My happy moments turned into defeat.

Broken promises,

Continuous let downs,

But all I want is for my mom to stick around.

So I endure it,

Time and time again,

Just to have her in my life,

But I never knew it would cause me so much strife.

Eventually,

I grew tired and couldn't take it anymore,

But I wasn't prepared for what lie in store.

I wouldn't see her again for another four years,

And the reunion would be full of tears.

More family to meet and get to know,

Hopefully from this moment we could grow.

But while on the outside,

Everything looked good,

On the inside,

I was still being misunderstood.

I thought we would be one big happy family,

But that couldn't be,

Too much time had separated us,

And attitudes and opinions had been formed.

The damage couldn't be repaired,

Alliances had been built,

And anger had built up.

Love was all I wanted,

To be nurtured and cared for was my only dream,

But you can't get a mother out of a person stuck in their

teens.

Do I love her?

Should I care?

Why does she deserve my loyalty when she's never been

there?

I have a heart,

I can't be that mean,

I still love her,

Even though my dream would never be complete.

I can't let you in,

I can't let you too close,

I have to love you from a distance,

In order to move on.

You taught me how to be a mother in reverse,

And for that,

I am blessed.

A mother/daughter relationship we may never have,

But at least my mind and heart can rest.

<u>Mother</u>

What is the definition of a mother?

Are you automatically declared one because you gave birth?

Or does the heart have to endure a few tears, pain and hurt?

Late nights with a sick child are not described in Webster's

Dictionary,

Neither are the bumps and bruises,

Or cuts and scrapes from your son trying to pull a Hail Mary.

Girl Scouts,

Cub Scouts,

Football and cheerleading practice,

All these events you must attend,

Even when you're tired, exhausted, or have a headache,

You must still pretend.

Pretend that you're okay,

When man has failed you and the bills are due.

Pretend you're alright,

When on the inside you're sad and blue.

If you hurt,

They hurt,

So you got to stay strong,

Hold up the front,

Until you're all alone.

Then the tears flow,

And this no one sees,

But every mother can relate,

To crying from having so much on their plates.

Motherhood is a full time job that never stops,

From conception to death,

A mother is on duty when there's no one else.

Sometimes unappreciated until it's too late,

We still bear crosses day to day.

Mother,

The nurturer of the family,

And though we endure a lot,

The rewards of this title never stop.

So accept it with grace and love,

For our strength and blessings come from above.

<u>Tears of a Mother</u>

After nine years,

You would think that I would have a handle on this

parenting thing,

But somehow,

I have changed.

Some for good and some for bad,

Somewhere down the road,

I lost myself.

Trying to be what others thought I should be,

I lost my own identity.

And it's taken me six years to realize that I haven't gained

it back,

And that's why I'm stuck where I'm at.

Currently defined by everyone else's version of me,

Needing to rediscover myself and bring back the old me.

My smile,

My sense of humor,

My enjoyment of life,

They all need to make a comeback in a hurry,

Because in life,

Nobody likes feeling like a burden.

A good mother is what I strive to be,

Don't talk about my problems because they usually get

thrown back in my face,

So I usually hold them all in and pray for a break.

I don't let anyone too close because I'm afraid to trust,

Most people judge first and understand later and that's not

what's up.

So to understand me,

You must really dig deep,

Because my smiles hide my tears,

From the eyes of many.

But I will journey on because I have four reasons that I

must,

It will get better,

In that I have to trust.

In His Honor

Death has never been easy to deal with,

The crying,

The heartache,

The pain,

I know all too well.

See,

My big brother's life ended way too soon for me,

But I got to live on,

And let his spirit live through me.

So in his honor,

I will make better choices.

In his honor,

I will raise my children to the best of my ability.

In his honor,

I will provide at all costs.

Before a man fully gains my heart,

Your approval I will think of from the start.

A great young woman is what I strive to be,

And when I get there,

You smiling down on me from heaven,

Is all I want to see.

I love you Butch,

Rest on big brother

Growing Up

Knowing that all childish must one day pass is a sign of

growth,

Accepting responsibility for the things you have done is a

sign of maturity.

Changing the things that need fixing reflects accountability,

Leaving your past behind and journeying on shows you

have faith.

Putting all these things together reveals God's working,

And standing your ground shows commitment.

Each phase shows growth in your life,

For there's nothing better than growth in Christ.

Renewed Strength

Having a hard time finding a reason to keep going,

Back's against the wall,

Tears continually falling from your eyes,

You feel like you just want to die.

Giving up is an option,

But where will that lead?

You have to find some source of strength,

Some source of motivation to keep on living,

Because blessings are all God keeps giving.

Trust Him with everything,

Step back and let go,

For what's best for you,

God already knows.

<u>Confused</u>

Have you ever been in love?

Or at least thought you were?

Not realizing you are confusing love with lust,

Infatuation with admiration.

Never knowing the true meaning of love,

Because you have never felt loved.

Exposing your heart to every man you meet,

Hoping that one of them will somehow make your life

complete.

Ending up with several children by different men,

Searching for love time and time again.

Afraid to be alone and face yourself,

So you sacrifice your body hoping that it helps.

Telling your past failures and sex escapades to a man

hoping to build a bond,

Not realizing you are getting the opposite reaction of what

you want.

So you shut down and bottle your feelings deep inside,

As the pain and hurt fills up the wells of your eyes.

Your reputation precedes you everywhere you go,

How to escape from your past,

You just don't know.

You want to be loved and feel those joys,

Trying to keep from being another man's toy.

Taking it day by day,

Trying to better you,

Repairing each piece of you,

Until the woman that was once there is no longer left.

Although you are confused,

You refuse to give in,

Your heart will be repaired,

Your soul will be healed.

You will love yourself,

And find love within,

And only then can the process of loving someone else

begin.

Road Block

What is a road block?

Is it meant to hinder you?

Or is it meant to provoke you to make a change?

I've had many road blocks in my thirty years of life,

Even some that I felt weren't right.

Like the situation with my daughter Eniyah,

Or the deaths of my aunt Tania,

My nephew Ronquez,

My big sister Dinky,

My great aunt Rochelle,

Or my big brother Butch.

But each situation taught and is still teaching me

something.

My road blocks are my stepping stones to my comeback,

My stepping stones to my breakthrough.

So you can cry,

Throw a pity party,

Or you can learn a lesson,

Realize where your strength comes from,

And embrace your road block,

The choice is up to you.

Danielle

Queen of the house,

Beautiful both inside and out,

Just starting to grab a hold of what life's all about.

Determined to finish anything I start,

Animalistic when I'm angry,

Nice to a certain extent,

Intelligent; my mind is my defense,

Educated; yet still willing to learn.

Loving when it comes to my kids,

Listener; everyone's issues seem to come

across these ears,

Enjoyable; I love to have a good time.

A woman,

A mother in every sense of the word,

The love I have for my children these days is unheard.

A best friend,

A lover,

Once you've had me,

You won't want another.

A woman learning to be true to herself,

Accomplishing the impossible is all that's left.

Life's Lessons

A Mother's Point of View

From conceiving a baby to carrying a child to maturity,

The journey to birthing a child has never been easy.

Labor pains and tears,

They quickly drift away,

The very first time,

You see your darling child's face.

Crawls and falls,

Bumps and bruises,

You're there for every moment.

Standing tall,

When dad has dropped the ball,

You give up?

No, not at all.

Breathing new life into your child when they feel defeated,

But your pain and hurt is kept a secret.

No child support,

No time spent with their child,

No phone calls,

No support shown at all.

But a mother can't quit,

She must journey on,

Making up where dad is lacking and slacking,

To see their child as a success is their only dream.

A protector,

A provider,

A nurturer,

A listener,

Everything a young child needs.

So mothers although it's hard,

Don't complain,

Just continue on,

And be what your child needs you to be.

The Parenting Journey

Until I became a parent,

I did not know about endurance.

First moments,

Enjoying those beautiful smiles,

Being strong when your heart is burdened down,

Smiling every time that child is around.

A lot of listening ears,

Yet very little solid advice,

Never having a dry pillow to lay my head on at night.

High as a mountain,

Yet low as a valley,

Continuing on,

Not knowing which way to turn,

Like standing alone in a dark alley.

Beautiful sunrises,

Beautiful sunsets,

Time in between slips away like magic.

Like preparing for a trip,

And not knowing what to pack.

A gentle breeze like a kiss from the wind,

Granting peace and endurance until the end.

Sweet laughter,

The comfort of a hug,

Treating bruised knees,

A gentle measure of love,

Healing the heart,

Like a band aid from above.

Children

Children can be a lot of things and bring several emotions.

Children bring joy, sadness, happiness, and sometimes hurt,

But in the end,

They are definitely worth the birth.

Sure there are many tears,

And my oldest has only been on this Earth for nine years.

Crying while they are asleep because their dads just walked

away,

But to them I must appear strong,

In order for them to make it day to day.

Children will push you to your limits,

My seven year old has ADHD and there isn't a calm bone

in him.

Can you really handle all the drama that children can

sometimes bring?

You see my six year old,

She's a drama queen.

And those sleepless nights,

Just a little while back,

My one year old couldn't get her days and nights right.

She hasn't completely figured it out yet,

And those diapers sure stink when they're not wet!

Children bring ups and downs,

Tears and smiles,

But through love,

Every day is worthwhile.

I love you

Eniyah, Te'Ontez, Danterryia, & Da'Nae

Parent

The definition of a parent is unclear to some,

Many out there think it's all games and fun.

At birth a bond is formed then until the end,

But you are supposed to be that child's parent,

Not their friend.

You can't dress like your child and then call yourself a

parent,

Put on some clothes,

Give them something to respect.

Men running in and out,

Come on now,

What's that all about?

Respect your kids,

Let alone yourself,

Teach them to value themselves,

If nothing else.

And it's more to life than name brands,

How about learning something in school?

And what about giving your children an example to follow?

Make your kids want to show you off.

Your time to be a child/teen ended the day you had a baby,

No ifs, ands, buts, or maybes.

So step up and accept your job,

And stop leaving society to raise your children.

Love your kids and yourself,

And be a parent to them,

If nothing else.

Pain

My heart feels pain,

That type of mental pain that you just can't change.

The type of pain that you hide deep within,

And put a smile on your face just to pretend.

Your feelings hurt,

So mentally you are exhausted,

But how to respond with love,

You were never taught it.

Constantly reliving the good times,

Cause this person you sincerely miss,

Battling anger because you're truly pissed.

A never ending battle daily,

My hurt feelings plague me.

Trying to show you that I am human too,

Hoping to convey that I have emotions as well as you.

But mentally I'm in pain,

I chose to trust,

So internalizing my feelings,

My highs and lows,

Is a must.

Refusing to let anyone else be called a friend,

I won't allow my trust to be abused again.

The pain of wanting to be happy for you and mad for

myself,

Has ruined the chances for anyone else.

The True Definition of a Man

What is a man?

Are you a man just because you are born a male?

Or do your mind, soul, and spirit have to go through some

things before a true man can prevail?

A true man provides for his family by any means,

To see them living comfortable is his only dream.

You were more than my brother,

You were the first real life example of a man that I have

seen.

You looked after me even when I pushed you away,

In my life,

You were determined to stay.

You taught me that a man should provide and treat me like

a queen,

Then you lead by example.

When I resisted,

You taught me the hard way.

I learned to be a better mother and to provide for my

children,

By watching you strive to provide for our entire family.

You were and still are our everything,

And losing you feels like a bad dream.

But I know in order to make you proud,

I have to continue to live on.

So each day as the tears continue to fall,

I will hold you close,

And know that God needed you more.

Big brother,

Watch over me from heaven,

Continue to send your love down,

Because I'm lost without you around.

I love you big brother Juan and I pray that one day this

won't hurt so bad…

You Live On

Your life to others may seem minute,

But to me your life serves as a truth.

I watched you stumble and fall,

But through your mistakes,

You held your head high and stood tall.

You were the best mother in my eyes,

You accepted your wrongs and never hid behind your

pride.

As your little sister,

I watched you give back and struggle to be the twinkle in

your children's eyes.

You showed me that it was okay to crawl,

Sometimes even completely fall,

But don't stay there,

Pick yourself up,

Dust it off,

Get back on life's ride.

Your journey taught me so much,

And just when I think life's too rough,

I think of you,

And remember nothing is too tough.

You are Superwoman in my heart,

And not even death can keep us apart.

Rest on big sister Dinky,

The woman I become is all because of you.

Gone but Never Forgotten

You're gone but never forgotten,

Your spirit lives on,

And today on your birthday,

I know a smile on your family's face is all that you would

want.

Your smile,

Your personality,

The love you gave out is honestly all this day is about.

The joy for life that you possessed is what keeps us holding

on,

The happiness you brought to our lives is what keeps us

strong.

Today is the day we celebrate your life,

Your accomplishments,

Your legacy,

And hold on to the lessons you taught us with all our might.

Rest in peace big brother Juan and happy birthday…

Hard Decisions

What are you to do when your back is against the wall,

And the decision you have to make is one that breaks your

heart?

You know that you have to do it,

There's nothing you can do with

this situation,

But just the thought of it has your poor little heart aching.

This choice is the only way they will get better,

But you are trying so hard to keep your family together.

The short term pain enveloped in lots of suffering and rain,

Is in no comparison to the joy the outcome will bring.

Your family's success has to worth you enduring the strain.

So as much as you don't want to do what is required of

you,

This decision will allow them to reach their full potential,

And that is worth a sacrifice from you.

Hold on tight to God's unchanging hand,

And know that things will get better in the end.

Misguided Truth

Who will step in on your behalf,

Comfort you in the times of sorrow,

Be there for you when you feel like there's no tomorrow?

Who can you depend on when you don't have a friend?

Who will hold you down until the very end?

Some say their mother,

Some say their man,

Some say their children,

Some say their best friend.

But I have to disagree,

While it is true,

These people may have been there for you,

The only person to continuously be there,

Lives on for eternity.

See,

Man will let you down,

Man will make you mad,

Man will drop the ball,

Man will make you sad.

But God can pick you up,

Wipe away all your tears,

Put joy back in your life,

Year after year.

So while man can be a great friend,

Remember in the end,

God will be your only true friend.

Just Live

Your life is a mess,

All in shambles,

All of your problems,

You feel you can't handle.

Constantly crying,

Trying to hide your pain,

Your spirit feels totally drained.

You've tried to do all that you can,

Feeling all alone and deserted again.

But I deny the charge,

This is just a test,

You see,

My God is not through with you yet.

While it may seem hard,

And you don't know what to do,

Turn it over to the master,

He will make a way for you.

So fall on your knees,

Pray your way through,

Have a little faith,

He word never fails,

It's tried and true.

Give Him some praise,

Not just now but as you go through,

And live,

That all you have to do!

Troubled Minds

A mind troubled is a mind that can't rest,

A mind filled with worry, heartache, and stress.

Smiling to hide the pain deep inside,

But those who really know you,

Know that's a lie.

You can't enjoy life,

You can't get these things off of your mind,

But if you just live in the moment,

You will realize that you have wasted a lot of time.

You see,

Most things that you are worried about haven't even

occurred,

You can't smile because of something you imagined.

Most of the time your mind is troubled for no reason at all,

So stop stressing,

Stop worrying,

Stop crying your heart out at night,

Just enjoy these precious moments,

And while you are at it,

Have a ball.

Struggles

Everyone struggles at some point in their lives,

Everyone must experience a little struggle and strife.

Struggles humble us,

They teach us a lesson,

But when many of us go through,

We tend to begin stressing.

But struggles are only temporary,

They don't last always,

There are brighter days not far away.

So dance,

Shout,

Praise your way through,

How long your struggles last,

Are up to you.

Hard Times

In life we all fall on hard times,

At some point in time,

But do we get up,

Or just lay there and cry?

Sometimes we cause our own hard times,

Being hardheaded and refusing to listen,

We halt our blessings,

When we stop going in the direction that God has us

headed.

Some cry,

Some pray,

Some even try to run away,

But your problems are always there waiting when you

return.

Some hard times come as lessons,

Lessons meant to teach you something in life,

So pouting won't do you any good,

God may be teaching you something,

Or punishing you for something you did.

Either way,

You need what He has for you,

So instead of being mad,

Embrace the hard times,

Just do what you are supposed to do,

And then maybe some of those hard times will ease up.

__Misery__

Misery loves company,

So why be a fool?

Why let them bring you down,

And make you miserable too?

They are unhappy and can't enjoy life,

So they want to make sure nothing in your life goes right.

Always wanting to hear your problems and drama,

So they can have something to gossip about.

Can't figure out what's wrong with their life,

But your wrong doings they know all about.

Don't let miserable people drag you down,

Enjoy your life and continue to smile.

<u>Loyalty</u>

Loyalty is a word misunderstood by many,

See,

Being loyal means being there through thick and thin,

Real loyalty has no end.

Whether keeping your secrets or just having your back,

True loyalty never lacks.

Being loyal means being non-judgmental,

Loyal friends support,

They never hinder.

A loyal friend has your best interests at heart,

And helping you become a better you,

Is their only goal from the start.

<u>No Instructions</u>

In school,

When taking a test,

You are given a pencil and instructions,

And told to do your best.

The night before,

You are told to go to bed early,

To ensure that you get plenty of rest.

Eat a healthy breakfast so your mind will be right,

According to your teachers,

These tests prepare you for life.

But in life,

There are plenty of tests and trials,

And they come with no instructions or guides,

Just road blocks and hurdles,

Bumps and bruises,

Rises and falls,

These tests require you to run, walk, and sometimes even

crawl.

But we were granted a few free passes in life,

Prayer,

Faith,

And God,

Are tools you need to ace the exam of life.

You may fail or flunk a few courses,

But each time you redo the lesson,

You learn something new.

Although we weren't given instructions to pass,

We were given tools to use,

So put your faith in my God,

And He will see you through.

No Greater Reward

Tears,

Physical pain,

Strength,

And endurance,

Tidal waves of emotion,

An up and down rollercoaster,

Highs and lows,

Fears hidden behind tears,

But a beacon of strength in front of you.

Weak at moments,

But not willing to give up,

The responsibility of you,

I placed on me.

But the joy I feel when you reach a milestone,

I can't explain.

Whether it's crawling,

Walking,

Or using the pot,

Or

Learning a hard math problem,

Or spelling your very long name,

Or

Tying your shoe,

Or sitting still for a few minutes regardless of your ADHD,

Or

Appreciating my sacrifices,

Like my long nights,

Or the tears,

Or stepping up when dad walked away,

No longer wanting to be there.

But there is no better reward than knowing that I am

responsible for four lives,

Shaping them and molding them,

And watching them grow,

They are my greatest rewards,

And without them,

I wouldn't exist.

A Little Less

No one knows what it takes to walk in my shoes,

No one understands just what it takes to keep a smile on my

face,

How about a little less judgment,

And a little more patience.

A little less heartache,

And a little more smiling faces.

A little less messiness,

And a little more encouraging words.

A little less drama,

And a little more joy.

Think of yourself a little less,

And consider others a little more.

For when you do this,

You will begin to see,

That this world is much bigger than you and me.

A Mother's Fears

The day I looked at each of you as you were born,

Joy and fear both consumed me.

Your lives given to me to guard,

So much happiness filled my heart.

The moment I looked into your eyes,

Nothing else mattered in life.

But as each of you grew,

So too did I.

My eyes opened up and I began to realize,

You were watching my every move,

And your life would chronicle mine,

If I didn't fight to stay alive.

So fear overtook me,

And from my responsibilities,

I tried to run.

But God is always there,

When you feel like there is no one.

He instilled a strength in me,

And a will to fight,

Yes,

The journey is hard,

And no,

Things won't change overnight,

But He told me to continue on,

Endure until the end,

A real mother never quits.

So time after time,

I pick myself up over and over again,

Cause even when I'm down,

God is still holding my hand,

Give them to Him,

And continue to fight,

Cause weeping only endures for a night.

A New Tomorrow

Yesterday,

I was lost,

But today,

I am found.

My feet have been placed on solid ground.

Yesterday,

I was drowning in my tears,

But today,

I am rejoicing in joy.

I know I have a reason to smile.

Yesterday,

I was only able to see my burdens,

But today,

I am able to see me overcoming.

Nothing the devil throws at me can keep me down.

You see,

I didn't know who I was,

Or where I belonged,

But then Jesus came along.

He showed me that I can be redeemed,

And of this day,

I have constantly dreamed.

Yesterday,

Is my past,

But today,

Is my new tomorrow.

To Have Loved

The greatest joy in life is to have loved and to be loved back,

To explore a person's most intimate thoughts,

To open your heart without fear of it being broken.

To have loved is to reveal your soul,

Give of yourself and not expect anything in return.

To have loved me,

Is in turn to have loved you.

For in order to love me,

You must first love you,

And for me,

The same is true.

The test of a man's character is the love of his heart,

To have loved and be loved means your character pricked

one's heart and you left your mark.

Through Thine Eyes

Look through my eyes,

And you will see life from my point of view.

A mother scared for history to repeat,

So she worries,

Constantly determined to not become her mother.

Wanting to be there for everything,

Because no one was ever there for her.

Afraid of letting her children down,

Because she was continuously let down,

And still feels as if she still is.

Afraid to be loved,

So she uses her kids as a clutch.

She won't let anyone in because the pain of the past hurts too

badly.

Trying to protect them from the terrors of this world,

Not knowing who to trust,

Scared to be away from them,

Because no one will treat them like me.

Crying your heart out because you feel like a failure at times,

Not fully understanding the concept of parenting,

Yet,

Not willing to give up on my kids.

Very defensive when I feel like my parenting skills are in

doubt,

Like a pit bull caged in.

A wounded child trying to be a mother,

Hurt,

Heart bleeding,

But still refusing to give up.

If I'm not good at anything else,

I will be the best mother I can be.

Look through my eyes and you will see,

A struggling mother determined to be the best she can be.

<u>Through Thine Eyes Pt. 2</u>

Look through my eyes and you will see,

Life through my telescope.

A child searching for my place in this world,

Scared and afraid,

Wanting to be loved at any cost.

Trying to please my mom,

Hoping to entice my dad to be a part of my life,

Wondering what I didn't do right.

Body constantly growing and changing,

Confused trying to figure it out.

Punishments,

Belts,

Rules,

Friends,

School,

Sports,

So much going on around me,

So much responsibility.

When am I allowed to be a kid?

I just want to play.

Run around outside in the rain and just enjoy the day.

Don't let me grow up too fast,

Then you'll wish I was a kid again.

Savor these moments,

For time waits for no man.

Through Thine Eyes Pt. 3

Look through my eyes and you will see,

Just what it takes to be me.

A man lost,

Trying to find himself.

Never had a man to guide me,

And teach me the way of life.

Out here slinging dick left and right because you think that

makes you a man,

Looking for love in a woman,

The love you never had.

Producing child after child,

But taking care of none.

No job,

Trying to hustle,

Because you were taught that's how a real man provides.

Kids neglected,

In and out of jail,

Rap sheet longer than a football field,

Searching for what you never had.

More lives destroyed,

When if you needed help,

All you had to do was ask.

<u>Through Thine Eyes Pt.4</u>

Journey into my world,

See life through my eyes.

Evaluate what it takes to be me,

And you will be surprised.

A woman searching for love,

Cause my daddy was never there.

A man lost,

Because no one ever cared.

Hearts broken,

Praying to be fixed.

Trust destroyed,

From so many let downs.

Trying to love you,

When I don't know how to love myself.

A hopeless case at times,

Willing to cater to you,

But when will I work on me?

A broken lover,

Willing and wanting to be loved,

Lost,

Afraid and confused,

But for you,

I'm willing to do what I have to do.

Love me first,

Then I can love you.

A Daughter's Apologies

What makes one a mother?

Is it birthright?

Or does raising a child make you a mother?

For me,

The latter is true.

So mama (Ms. Joyce),

This one is for you!

You took me in and raised me as your own,

And for that,

My heart you will forever own.

You treated me no different,

You loved me the same,

But as I got older,

Things started to change.

I grew the big head,

I thought I knew it all,

You tried to steer me right,

But at the time,

Deaf ears were what it fell upon.

I bucked you,

I fought on numerous occasions,

But you never stopped loving me.

But you stood your ground,

And had me locked up.

But even through this,

Your love grew tough.

I still gave you hell,

And I refused to back down,

But you had reinforcements knock me down.

You wouldn't let up,

But your love stayed strong,

And over the years,

Our bond has grown.

I felt bad for all the things I had put you through,

Because deep down,

I loved you more than even you knew.

My heart broke,

For every time that I had made you cry,

I would trade my life for yours in a heartbeat,

Anything to make it right.

As I grow as a mother,

I realize you are full of love,

And when God created you,

He released an angel from above.

I apologize for the hurt and pain I caused you,

I am now and will forever be grateful for you.

A Mother's Apology

What did I know?

So young and confused,

Thinking I could trap a man,

By giving birth to you.

Lost,

Searching for love,

Playing a dangerous game.

But once you were born,

Everything changed.

I found a new love,

A new reason to live,

But mistakes were still made.

Trying to be the best mother to you,

Yet still trying to find someone to love me.

I allowed man after man to enter my life,

Collecting baggage,

And inadvertently abandoning you.

Trying to manage motherhood and a love life,

Struggling but not willing to quit,

I will rise to the occasion,

My best is what you'll get.

I apologize for any pain I brought to you,

But I promise my all to you.

Any mistakes I've made,

I own up to,

But from this moment on,

I will make it up to you.

Love's Mysteries

A Love Lost

If I ever loved you,

Then you had to know that I once trusted you.

But when you left,

I became disgusted in you.

I refuse to do the things I used to do with you,

With my new boo.

And although I'm hurt,

I shall get through.

A Lonely Heart

Why?

Why can't they understand,

That all I want is the true love of a man?

Yeah,

I know I have a lot on my plate,

Four kids,

Being a single parent,

And hardly any time for dates.

But I deserve love too,

Someone who sees the good in me,

And wants to add to.

But I know it's not my choice,

I must wait for the one that God has picked out for me,

But I must admit,

It's a long, hard journey.

I'm a good woman,

And I just want someone who appreciates me.

My sacrifices,

My dedication,

My love,

And my loyalty,

To take all that I give,

And treat me like a queen.

The heart wants what it wants,

And right now,

Mine wants love and companionship.

So as bad as it hurts,

I will sit and wait,

For my heart won't be lonely always.

Miss Me (A Woman's Ode)

Miss me with your lame excuses,

Your lies you continue to tell,

Playing on my emotions,

And my dream of falling in love.

Miss me with your act,

Playing innocent,

Like you ain't done anything wrong,

Trying to persuade me with your words,

Hoping that I'm just naive enough to believe nothing that

I've heard.

Miss me with your talks of another chance,

Cause I'm tired of all your bull,

And I have no time for playing.

Miss me when I'm gone,

For you lost a good thing,

But for now,

I plan to wait until God sends me the one presents me my

ring…

And completes all my dreams.

Love's Praises

When it falls on me,

I feel so much joy deep inside,

Your love causes me to feel alive.

It woke up a part of me frozen long ago,

And the more it reveals itself,

The stronger our love grows.

The most beautiful thing in life is to love and be loved back.

The love we share cannot be destroyed because it's so pure,

This is that "real love" that Mary sang about,

And of that I'm sure.

That love that Smokey Robinson crooned about,

That love that Mariah couldn't live without.

That kind of love that brings about a change,

You know the kind that has your friends saying you are

acting strange.

This love has me dancing on clouds,

And I never want to come down.

I waited,

And my wish was granted,

You,

My King,

Me,

Your Queen.

So together,

Hand in hand,

We shall enjoy our journey and complete each other's

dreams.

Dedicated To:

My Future Husband

The Eye of the Storm

It was beautiful at first,

All smiles, cuddles, and kisses,

Constantly holding hands,

And always referring to me as the Mrs.

But along the way,

Things began to change,

And priorities were rearranged.

You became distant,

While resisting being intimate.

Phone calls no longer being answered,

And hugs were a thing of the past.

Continuously telling me our love hasn't changed,

But daily,

I'm feeling more and more shortchanged.

Spinning round and round with the more lies you tell,

Imprisoned in my mind's jail cell.

I got to escape this storm before it becomes a tornado and

destroys everything in it's' path,

I can't continue to stay.

So before death consumes me,

I must walk away.

Now comes the hurt, heartache, and pain,

But I have to endure because the sun is somewhere shining

even when it rains.

<u>What Changed</u>

You were a dream come true,

Or so I thought,

My heart fluttered at the sight of you,

But suddenly,

We stopped.

My emotions no longer mattered,

You were too busy chasing skirts,

You had a good woman,

But all you wanted to do was flirt.

Telling me I was loved,

Knowing it was all lies,

I tried to hold on,

But I constantly asked myself why?

What changed between us?

What turned my dreams into nightmares?

Although it hurts,

I know I'm better off,

If you're not here.

What changed with you?

I may never know,

But I must let go,

In order to continue to grow.

Bruises of My Heart

Wounded,

Bleeding internally,

Constantly searching for reprieve.

Deep puncture wounds,

Causing pain to flow,

Time and time again,

Open wounds fester and grow.

No Band-Aid big enough to fix this booboo,

Heart scarred,

Feelings fragile,

Crying out for relief.

My heart's suffering causes mental anguish,

And feelings of being caged in an emotional jail cell.

When will it end?

When will my heart be repaired?

Can I really escape the scars placed on my heart?

Or were they put there as learning lessons meant to guide me

along love's journey?

Either way,

Love still exists and so must I,

Bruised or not,

My heart keeps me alive.

Keeping Secrets

A relationship without trust is destined to fail,

That's like the head being led by the tail.

Like a house built on sand,

A relationship full of lies will quickly wash away.

Hidden secrets are no different than bold face lies,

Each of these will only destroy what you think you have.

Lying to her to pacify her only further degrades her,

And she's so clueless that she doesn't realize she's being

blinded by his lies.

And when she finally opens her eyes to realize she's been a

pawn in his little mind game,

Her heart is broken and she is feeling ashamed.

But the test is just now beginning,

For he is truly not winning.

But now she's angry and hurt and wants him to feel her pain,

Going from man to man,

Constantly telling lies,

Unwilling to commit,

Not realizing she's changed.

Becoming the same thing she despised,

Carrying around extra baggage,

On the outside she appears to be hard,

But on the inside she's scarred.

Hiding from her pain,

She's subconsciously given him control,

But if she was wise,

She would realize,

He wasn't hers from the beginning.

Games are not a part of God's design,

And your heart is not a toy.

Keeping secrets produces a domino effect,

And each person's heart becomes suspect.

But hold on,

Stand your ground,

Don't budge on your standards,

And in the end,

He'll be the one left with regrets.

New Beginning

Amazing feelings,

As I entertain the idea of getting to know you.

Wondering where will it go,

Pondering if you will remain true.

Smiling because my heart flutters at the thought of you,

Rejoicing in the fact that my smile has returned.

A new beginning,

A brand new experience,

Scared yet excited at the same time.

Just letting it flow,

Allowing it to go at its' own pace,

Where will it end?

Only God knows.

Once Upon a Time

My heart,

My soul,

My other half,

Because of you,

I know our love will last.

I never knew real true love before you,

And now my heart is consumed with a burning desire for

you.

At the sound of your voice,

My heart skips a beat,

I can't wait until we finally meet.

You genuinely make my heart smile,

And when I think of you,

On the inside I feel like a little child.

You are a prize to me,

You the only man that I see.

You truly are a dream come true,

I would be honored to marry you.

My king,

My knight in shining armor,

To be your woman is such an honor.

A young man with a very mature mind,

You are surely worth every minute of my time.

Thinking of you fills my life with happiness,

Your love washed away all my sadness.

Our love will endure through it all,

Good or bad,

I don't care,

I'm going to love you regardless of who gets mad.

I will continue to place my heart in your hands,

And I will continue to love you,

My heart,

My soul,

My friend,

My man.

My Dream

My dream came true when I met you,

Now without you in my life,

I don't know what to do.

I dreamed that I would meet a man,

Who would take my heart?

Caress it,

And hold it carefully in the palm of his hands.

I dreamed that this man would treat me like a queen,

He would complete my heart, soul, and dreams.

He would constantly make me smile,

Not just on my face,

But smile from the heart making it all worthwhile.

But unfortunately,

He wasn't the one,

He left my heart broken and the job undone.

So I have embellish my dream,

Start over from scratch,

To see what can be achieved.

Love's Canvas

A man with many troubles and struggles,

A man who thought he had lost his self,

A man who thought he couldn't be loved by another.

A man who cried his self to sleep at night,

His true feelings,

He is not willing to uncover.

But through all this tragedy,

Love was discovered.

Now a man with a soul,

This new feeling of happiness,

He can't seem to control.

He now knows the true meaning of joy,

On the inside,

He's like a little boy with a brand new toy.

When you look at him,

You should see a king,

Because he has become a factor,

He's walking into his destiny.

He's becoming everything he's destined to be,

He is finally completing my current dreams.

<u>Love Inspires</u>

Love will inspire change,

Love will make you do things that can be considered strange.

Love will force you to make those hard decisions,

Those kinds of choices that bring tears to your eyes in the

end.

Love warms your heart,

When you've been hurt and you feel like you can't go on,

Love builds you up where you are weak,

It restores you,

It makes you strong.

Love creates smiles,

When on the inside your heart is breaking,

Love creates peace,

When it feels like your world is shaking,

Love calms the storm.

Love endures all things,

The good and the bad.

Whether laughing or crying,

Knowing that love is present is inspiring.

All things work together for my good,

And with love,

My soul feels good.

A Glimpse of Hope

Just,

With you everyone gets a fair chance.

Encouraging,

Always coaching me to reach my full potential.

Resilient,

Determined to bounce back no matter the circumstances.

Exhortative,

Meaning you are the most reassuring man I know.

Masculine,

Your presence defines being a man.

Inhibited,

With the right woman there is no limit to where your love

will go.

Accepting,

Looking past my flaws and taking me for who I am.

Honest,

Telling it like it is regardless if it's accepted or rejected.

A man full of love,

One whom I once loved and cherished,

The love of my life at one point,

My soul mate.

But things changed somewhere down the line,

You weren't the man I envisioned in my mind.

But at least I experienced feelings beyond belief,

Soaking up knowledge like a tree.

Better luck next time,

Hopefully the next one is designed to be mine.

Invisible Touch

Have you ever had a mental connection without physical

interaction?

Mental intimate stimulation causing mental ejaculation of

your thoughts,

Visions of them in your dreams that you can't stop.

Happiness at the mention of their name,

Since they came into your life,

Nothing has been the same.

Your mind, body and soul they have conquered,

To be considered theirs,

You would be honored.

As each thought of them crosses your mind,

You envision spending nothing but quality time.

Your hearts are forever intertwined,

And you pledge your love and loyalty to them until the end

of time.

Up to You

How many have been in love and messed it up before?

Either you didn't trust,

Or you were too selfish to surrender fully to love,

Afraid from past hurts and relationship failures,

Or just not willing to open up.

But somehow you get another chance at love,

There's actually a person willing to take a chance on you.

You must first decide if you are going to take control,

Or just surrender and let the opportunity go.

Me personally,

I done messed up in love before,

And I don't want to mess it up anymore.

I'm going to sit back and follow your lead,

Allow you to run the show,

With you I feel security,

I can completely let go.

I'm going to stay out of my own way,

And leave it all up to you.

In this relationship,

You've paid the cost to be the boss.

Just by dealing with you've proven that you can handle a lot,

And for that,

The love between us will never stop.

I surrender my mind, heart, body, and soul,

This love is forever,

I'm not willing to let go.

<u>Floating</u>

Your love puts me in a place that I can't explain,

But the joy I feel has me not wanting a thing to change.

Envisioning your smile places me on cloud nine,

I'm so glad that you're all mine.

The sparkle in my eye that comes every time I hear your

name,

For these feelings of happiness,

You are to blame.

Constantly reminding me of just how beautiful I am,

Both inside and out,

Our love is built to last and that's without a doubt.

Whenever I think of you,

I feel like I'm riding an everlasting high,

The only day I will come down is my dying day,

Your love gives me the strength I need to get by.

Through the good and bad,

The ups and the downs,

I'm still going to be floating and not want to come down,

This love is surreal,

It has me feeling like I'm walking through the clouds.

You have me floating on thin air,

My life would be incomplete without you there.

Your love keeps me dedicated to you,

And until death separates me from you,

I pledge my dedication to the love built between us two.

Games They Play

The games they play are ridiculous,

They want you to smile when they tell jokes that play with

your heart.

You can't even front like your feelings are not hurt,

They show up on the outside,

You just can't hide them no matter how hard you try.

But to stay is a must,

I love you with all my heart,

In that you can always trust.

Now I might be mad for a while,

But I'm not going anywhere.

You are my heart and soul,

And arguments do happen,

But we can't live in the moment.

I'm going to say some things that you don't like,

And the same goes for you,

But during these times,

It's all in what we choose to do.

Do we go to bed angry?

Or do we apologize and make up?

We should never go to bed without saying I love you,

Because we can't just walk away if this love is true.

So let's not play games to see who can make who mad,

Let's not try to get under each other's skin.

Happy times with you are all that I want,

Because being with you until the end of time is my idea of

holding on.

To Feel Loved

Have you ever felt alone even around family?

Trying to feel the love of those around you,

But you are not one of the chosen few.

But out of respect,

You do what you should,

But in your eyes,

You feel like the love you give out is no good.

Just once if you could feel the same warmth of love as those

around you,

The things that little bit of love would do for you.

But you must suck it up and continue to live,

Ask God to teach you how to love in spite of,

All the love you need lies between God and your children.

So smile,

And know that God loves you from beginning to end.

Motivators to Live

An Earthly Angel

A loving woman,

An angel from above.

When God created you,

He showed the world a real life example of love.

My world was in shambles when I met you,

But you took me in and raised me as your own,

Even when I mistreated you and did you wrong.

You never gave up on me and you are still standing by my

side,

It is your strength that I gain from,

That knowledge is what keeps me alive.

See,

Motherhood does not come with guidelines,

But for every tear as a single mother,

You are right there to dry.

Even though you did not birth me,

To lose your love would hurt me.

I couldn't dream of a better woman to call my mother,

Your place could be filled by no other.

And as I look back over my teenage years,

And all the hell I caused,

I'm thankful that you never gave up at all.

The woman that stands here before me,

Is the mother that I inspire to be.

There are not enough words in the English language to

express how much I love and appreciate you,

So I will strive until my dying day,

Just to show you.

Mama,

You are my heart and soul,

I'm glad God blessed you to see another birthday,

And may He bless you with many more.

Dedicated to:

My Adopted Mother

Joyce (Bell) Smith

Blessing from God

This earth received a blessing when your mother gave birth

to you,

No one knew your life would touch so many.

Childhood may have been hard and you had your personal

struggles,

Even tried to run when God placed His calling on your life.

But I'm so glad that He wouldn't let you go,

But through you,

God is allowing me to grow.

See you serve a major purpose in this life,

You are a mother to those of us who feel motherless.

I know we seem so hardheaded and we don't listen and

sometimes you just want to give up on us,

But please don't.

For without you we would truly be lost.

We are behind you without a doubt,

Let you get in some trouble,

Watch how many of us come out.

We truly love you and are proud to say,

We have the most beautiful Queen in the nation.

Dedicated to:

My Pastor

Queen Bishop Ernestine Williams

<u>Eniyah</u>

My oldest daughter,

My princess,

My jewel,

The first one God gave to me.

Before you,

I couldn't really see,

How much a child could change me for the better.

Things felt so brand new,

The days I laid eyes on you.

My first born,

My princess,

My crown jewel,

My life changed for the better the day I had you.

Te'Ontez

My only son,

My prince,

My right hand man,

God knew what He was doing when He placed you in my

plans.

Free spirited,

Uninhibited,

An enjoyer of life,

I always imagined what a male version of me would be like.

Strong and brave,

Yet still mama's baby,

Even when you're afraid.

The prince of the house,

A future king,

I promise to show you how to treat a queen.

You are a boy by birth,

A young man at heart,

Destined to be great right from the start.

You my heart with one look at you,

Te'Ontez Ke'Don Bigsby,

I love you.

Danterryia

My second daughter,

A little diva in training,

Sparks from your personality are constantly raining.

A princess you are,

And definitely a jewel,

I'm so glad God blessed me with you.

Shy at first,

And afraid to talk,

Your Godmother was the only one that you did want.

Things have changed and your personality is blossoming

through,

They can no longer mention shy in the same sentence as you.

Staying cute and fly for you is a must,

And having plenty of swag is a plus.

I know you are going to be something major,

You're only six years old and you already have plenty of

haters.

But negativity has no place in your world,

God made you,

A powerful girl.

Smart,

Beautiful and talented,

I'm truly amazed,

In my heart is your special place.

Da'Nae (Before You Were Born)

Conceived in August,

Due in May,

What a wonderful blessing you are,

Miss Da'Nae.

Emotions on high at the thought of having you,

But blessed I am,

I know this much is true.

A very peculiar child while still in the womb,

One who will inspire change,

Also one that many people would label as strange.

But to be strange is a blessing from God,

Because His people are very different and they don't just fit

in,

You will stand out in crowds,

Yet God's love will shine through you,

A blessing you are and I'm glad to be the mother of you.

Da'Nae meaning she, who judges,

Is a beautiful name,

History and religion,

A name picked out just for you.

So as I await your journey into this world,

I can't help but smile,

Because I know that the spirit and glory of the Lord will be

inside my child.

So come on in and accept your place,

God has a purpose for you,

And time awaits....

Da'Nae

My last princess,

The "Little Miss Unexpected",

But the love you give me will never be rejected.

So full of life and joy,

Happiness and praise,

The smile you gave me can't be erased.

My happiest child by far,

I know you are destined to become a star.

A real blessing in disguise,

Through you,

God opened my eyes.

You were sent to save our family,

God's gift,

And to me,

Another chance to get it right.

A jewel that's for sure,

And because of you,

I know I can endure.

You have no idea of the impact you have on my life,

Pushing me to be a better mom.

One smile from you,

And I feel calm.

A star at some point in your life,

Everything about you,

God made in His light.

So shine bright my child,

You reap what you sow after while.

Bonus Material:

Cherish

The moment I met you,

I knew that you were the one for me.

You stood out from the rest,

Just the thought of you caused my heart to pound deep

within my chest.

Your smile lit up the room,

It gave me a new reason to live.

The love you brought to my world can be compared to

nothing I have ever felt before,

The moments we share,

Are as beautiful as the sight of the waves crashing against

the beach's shore.

I cherish the day we met,

The day that your love swept me off my feet.

But more than anything,

I cherish the fact that you love every inch of me.

www.ingramcontent.com/pod-product-compliance
Lightning Source LLC
Chambersburg PA
CBHW072001040426
42447CB00009B/1437